I DON'T COOK FOR KIDS.

FATHER-DAUGHTER DANCE '97

I DON'T COOK FOR KIDS.

Created and Published
TYNETTE JONES
2019

Copyright © 2019 by Tynette Jones

All rights reserved. No part of this book may be reproduced or used in any manner without written permission of the copyright owner except for the use of quotations in a book review. For more information, address: TynetteJones@gmail.com.

ISBN 978-0-578-22499-2 (paperback)

First Edition, 2019

www.IDontCookForKids.com

"HE SATISFIES THE THIRSTY AND FILLS THE HUNGRY WITH GOOD THINGS"

PSALMS 107:9 NLT

"SO GO AHEAD. EAT YOUR FOOD WITH JOY, AND DRINK YOUR WINE WITH A HAPPY HEART, FOR GOD APPROVES OF THIS!"

ECCLESIASTES 9:7 NLT

TABLE OF CONTENTS

PREFACE	8
INTRODUCTION	10

SMALL BITES — 13

ROSEMARY RUM SWEET POTATOES	15
SMOKED SALMON TOSTADA	17
SMOKED SALMON CROSTINI	18
APRICOT HONEY WHISKEY WINGS	21
SPICY ASIAN PEPPER'D WINGS	22
SMOKED COCONUT LIME WINGS	25

ENTREES — 26

WASABI SEAFOOD PIZZA	28
SPICY TURKEY BURGER and FRIES	32
SHRIMP CURRY NOODLES	37

CILANTRO FISH AND POBLANO RICE	39
SWEET PEPPER MEATBALL PASTA	43
WHOLE FISH AND MUSHROOM MARSALA COUSCOUS	46
RED WINE LAMB CHOPS/TACOS	53

DESSERTS 59

AVOCADO KEY LIME PIE	61
BOOZY MANGO PEACH COBBLER	62
DRUNKEN SLOPPY S'MORES	64
COCONUT LIME BASIL RUM CAKE	69

COCKTAILS 70

MARGARITA ON THE ROCKS	72
BERRY BASIL COCKTAIL	73
SMOKED ROSEMARY PEACH TEA	74

PREFACE

When I first began my culinary journey, I never imagined I would one day create my own cookbook. As a child, I always loved to eat, but anytime I was called to the kitchen to learn how to cook, my sentiment was always, "Just let me know when it's done." Why cook when I could just eat and enjoy the food instead. Most times, the irony in life usually turns out to be the best part of the journey. Long gone are the days of me not getting my hands dirty in the kitchen. Now, I like to chop it up, season it over, and drizzle it down with the best of them. From humble beginnings in my college apartment to the release of my first cookbook, cooking has become my love language of giving and an extension of my identity.

Like a lot of 20-something-year-olds, I thought I had to create myself, define who I was in society, and make great things happen in my own strength. Fast-forward to rounding out this last chapter in my twenties, I've come to realize a few things about identity. Identity was never meant to be created in our own strength; it was a blessing given to us before we were ever formed in our mother's womb. To know who you are and whose you are is to make an active choice to not only receive your identity, but to believe in it and walk in its truth every day.

I've heard many people say, "Time is more valuable than money," which I do believe to be true. However, I've concluded — identity is more valuable than time. As spiritual beings having a human experience, our identities have never been tied to the things of this world, it was never meant to be. Knowing who you are and whose you are enables you to harness the power that living in your identity affords, and therefore you won't waste your time on things (people, situations, etc.) you were never called to deal with in your own strength. Albert Einstein once said that time and space are relative to the observer. Now if we take this statement and apply its logic to the creator of the universe, the author of all time and space, then we must know that our identity not only holds the ultimate truth, it supersedes all constructs of this fickle world including time and space.

    Identity is eternal, it can never change, it will never change, and it cannot be damaged by circumstances, situations, or even at the hands of our own doing. Your identity is your birthright. You are a child of the Most High God, therefore you lack no good thing, not one! In your identity, you are loved, welcomed, accepted, heard, forgiven, redeemed, graced, covered, healed, protected, comforted, blessed, surely followed by goodness and mercy, saved, refreshed, set apart, encouraged, developed, instructed, strengthened, sharpened, improved, favored, equipped, fruitful, distinguished, respected, corrected, restored, perfected, aligned, refined, renewed, revived and radiant! You lack no good thing because all things are working together for your good. Let this truth penetrate your entire being. From your head to your toes, all the way down to the root of your soul, know whose you are and be true to yourself.

    So, why don't I cook for kids? Simply put, I don't have any. However, in the context of identity, I don't cook for kids because living a successful life requires a spiritual maturity to conquer all negative emotions: fear, doubt, anxiety, guilt, discouragement, etc. Knowing whose you are should give you a boldness to know that all things are possible and the confidence to be about kingdom business because you have a divine assignment. It's not about mind over matter, it's knowing who you are and living in your identity each day. There used to be so many things I would constantly find myself worrying about. The irony of it all is that through all the worrying, I was always cooking and creating, never really considering the possibility that creating a cookbook could become a reality. Now here you are, reading the preface to my cookbook. I will admit, this whole experience kind of blows my mind. If I'd put the effort into knowing then, what I know now, then I would have known this was bound to happen sooner than later.

    Before you turn the page to recreate these delicious recipes, I encourage you to make a daily habit of cultivating a bold confidence in your identity. Know yourself, be accountable for your growth and unshakable in your identity. Know that you lack no good thing and that all things are working together for your good.

INTRODUCTION

In my kitchen, there are a few things I consider mandatory for every dish: fresh ingredients, bold flavor, and results that are simply delicious.

Fresh Ingredients

When I think of the word fresh, I think of something new and each ingredient plays an important role in creating something new. With each recipe, I've chopped, minced, diced, and sliced these fresh ingredients with one purpose in mind — creating something new.

"But forget all that — it is nothing compared to what I am going to do. For I am about to do something new. See, I have already begun! Do you not see it?"
Isaiah 43:18–19 NLT

"...Look, I am making everything new...Write this down, for what I tell you is trustworthy and true."
Revelations 21:5 NLT

Bold Flavor

Not for the bland of taste, food should be fun and worth every indulgent bite. Bold flavors entice the taste buds and leave a lasting impression on the tongue. The purpose of each recipe in this book is to create a bold, unforgettable ambience in your mouth.

"...we can now come boldly and confidently into God's presence...so you should feel honored"
Ephesians 3:12–13 NLT

Simply Delicious

Tried and true, these recipes have been thought of, inspired by, tested, tested some more, and then tested again. From tasting the first bite to savoring every crumb off the plate, good is easy — it's simply delicious!

"Taste and see that the Lord is good. Oh, the joys of those who take refuge in him!"
Psalms 34:8 NLT

What I enjoy most about these recipes is their versatility. Their different components can be applied to adaptations beyond what the recipe states. Let's start with the small bites for example. The mango pico de gallo used in the smoked salmon tostada recipe would be delicious over fried or baked whole fish, fish fillets, or chicken breast.

THE RED ONION JAM USED IN THE SMOKED SALMON CROSTINI RECIPE CAN ALSO BE SPREAD OVER A GOOD JUICY BURGER, LAMB CHOP OR CRACKERS WITH CHEESE. DRESS YOUR FAVORITE GRILLED VEGETABLES IN THE ASIAN PEPPER'D WING SAUCE OR PAIR THE SAUCE WITH THAI STYLE NOODLES OVER SHRIMP, CHICKEN OR LAMB.

 FOR THE ENTREES, THE HONEY WASABI SAUCE IN THE WASABI SEAFOOD PIZZA WOULD MAKE A GREAT SPREAD ON AN ASIAN-INSPIRED SANDWICH OR TACO. THE SHRIMP CURRY NOODLES, MINUS THE NOODLES, WOULD MAKE A DELICIOUS ETHNIC SAUSAGE DOG. I ENVISION A TOASTED, BUTTERED HOT DOG BUN, HOT ITALIAN SAUSAGE, GRILLED ONIONS AND BELL PEPPERS, THE SHRIMP CURRY SAUCE, GARNISHED WITH FRESH CILANTRO AND RED PEPPER FLAKES. THE MUSHROOM MARSALA COUSCOUS IS DELICIOUS OVER THE RED WINE LAMB CHOPS TOPPED WITH A LITTLE BIT OF LEMON ZEST, AND THE PEAR AND FENNEL MINT SLAW FROM THE RED WINE LAMB CHOPS SHOULD ALSO BE ENJOYED OVER SMOKED SALMON GARNISHED WITH RED PEPPER FLAKES AND A LITTLE HONEY TO TASTE.

 AS YOU RECREATE THESE RECIPES, I ENCOURAGE YOU TO EXPERIMENT WITH THE CULINARY POSSIBILITIES WITHIN EACH RECIPE. ALTHOUGH THIS COOKBOOK IS A PRODUCT OF MY CREATIVITY, THERE IS AN UNDERLYING IDENTITY IN THESE RECIPES WAITING TO BE BORN THROUGH THE FRUITS OF YOUR CREATIVITY. I HOPE YOU ENJOY CULTIVATING SOMETHING NEW WITH BOLD FLAVOR THAT IS SIMPLY DELICIOUS!

SMALL BITES

ROSEMARY RUM SWEET POTATOES

SMOKED SALMON TOSTADA

SMOKED SALMON CROSTINI

APRICOT HONEY WHISKEY WINGS

SPICY ASIAN PEPPER'D WINGS

SMOKED COCONUT LIME WINGS

ROSEMARY RUM SWEET POTATOES

Sweet potatoes baked then broiled in a brown sugar spiced rum glaze and garnished in fresh rosemary, walnuts and toffee bits.

INGREDIENTS:

- 6 sweet potatoes
- 2 tablespoons butter
- 2/3 cup brown sugar
- 2/3 cup dark spiced rum
- Chinese five spice powder
- 1 teaspoon nutmeg
- 1 teaspoon vanilla extract
- ½ teaspoon vanilla bean
- ¼ teaspoon ground ginger
- Fresh rosemary
- 1 orange, zest and juice
- Black pepper
- Sea salt
- Walnuts, chopped
- Toffee bits

DIRECTIONS:

Preheat oven to 400°F. Puncture sweet potatoes on all sides with a fork. Wrap each sweet potato in foil, bake until tender, 40-45 minutes.

Melt butter in small saucepan over medium heat. Add brown sugar, rum, 2 tablespoons Chinese five spice powder, nutmeg, vanilla extract, vanilla bean, ground ginger and two fresh rosemary sprigs. Bring to boil, stirring constantly (2-3 minutes). Remove from heat, discard rosemary sprigs, stir in orange zest and juice, set aside.

Unwrap sweet potatoes. Cut into halves lengthwise, place skin down on foil-lined cookie sheet. Gently mash each potato with a fork. Season with five spice, black pepper and salt to taste.

Brush generous amount of glaze on each half. Broil low on top rack until glaze is absorbed. Garnish with chopped rosemary, walnuts, and toffee bits.

SMOKED SALMON TOSTADA

Toasted tortilla topped with avocado spread, smoked salmon, spicy mango pico de gallo, and garnished with rosemary, chives, red pepper flakes and lime zest.

INGREDIENTS:

- Smoked salmon
- Tortillas, toasted
- Red pepper flakes
- Rosemary
- Chives
- Lime Zest

AVOCADO SPREAD

- 1 avocado
- 1 lime, zest and juice
- Black pepper
- Salt

MANGO PICO DE GALLO

- 2 honey mangoes, cubed
- 1 red bell pepper, diced
- 1 jalapeño, diced
- 1 lime, zest and juice
- ½ medium red onion, diced
- ½ cup cilantro, chopped
- ¼ teaspoon kosher salt
- ¼ teaspoon sugar

DIRECTIONS:

FOR THE AVOCADO SPREAD
Mash avocado, add lime zest and juice, black pepper and salt to taste, mix well. Set aside in refrigerator.

FOR THE MANGO PICO DE GALLO
Mix all ingredients, chill in refrigerator.

ASSEMBLE AND SERVE
Layer avocado spread on toasted tortilla, add smoked salmon and mango pico de gallo. Garnish with red pepper flakes, rosemary, chives and lime zest. Serve chilled.

SMOKED SALMON CROSTINI

Toasted bread topped with chive and onion cream cheese spread, smoked salmon, red onion jam, caviar, and garnished with thyme, cracked black pepper and lemon zest.

INGREDIENTS:

- Smoked Salmon
- Bread, thinly sliced and toasted
- Chive and onion cream cheese spread (Philadelphia brand)
- Salmon caviar
- Rosemary
- Thyme
- Cracked black pepper
- Lemon zest

RED ONION JAM

- Olive oil
- ½ red onion, diced
- 7-10 thyme sprigs, stems removed
- ¼ cup red wine vinegar
- ¼ cup brown sugar
- Black pepper
- Salt
- 1 lemon, zest

DIRECTIONS:

FOR THE RED ONION JAM
Heat olive oil in saucepan over medium heat. Add onions and thyme, cook covered until soft and fragrant (7-10 minutes).

Add red wine vinegar, increase heat to high. Add brown sugar, bring to boil, stir. Add black pepper and salt to taste, let boil (3-5 minutes), do not stir.

Remove from heat, stir in lemon zest, let cool to room temperature.

ASSEMBLE AND SERVE
Layer cream cheese spread on toasted bread, add smoked salmon, red onion jam and caviar.

Garnish with rosemary, thyme, cracked black pepper and lemon zest.

APRICOT HONEY WHISKEY WINGS

Baked chicken wings tossed in a tangy, sweet apricot honey whiskey sauce and garnished with red pepper flakes.

INGREDIENTS:

MARINADE
- 4 pounds chicken wingettes and drummettes
- Honey whiskey
- Coke
- Honey

RUB
- ¼ cup brown sugar
- 1 tablespoon black pepper
- 1 tablespoon kosher salt
- ½ teaspoon ground ginger

SAUCE
- 5 apricots, seeded and chopped
- 1 tablespoon butter
- ½ cup honey whiskey
- ¼ cup brown sugar
- 1/8 cup honey
- 1 tablespoon Worcestershire
- 1 tablespoon honey Dijon
- ½ teaspoon cayenne powder
- ½ teaspoon salt
- 1 lemon, zest and juice

DIRECTIONS:

FOR THE MARINADE
Mix equal parts honey whiskey and coke in a freezer bag. Add chicken, completely submerge in whiskey-coke mixture, marinate in refrigerator overnight.

Spray a foil-lined cookie sheet with cooking spray, set aside. Remove chicken from marinade, pat dry. Transfer chicken to cookie sheet, drizzle honey on both sides of chicken, set aside.

FOR THE RUB
Mix all rub ingredients together, generously season both sides of chicken, set aside.

FOR THE SAUCE
Preheat oven to 450°F.
Melt butter in saucepan over medium heat. Add all sauce ingredients (except lemon zest and juice), mix well, bring to boil, stir constantly. Process with immersion blender, or let sauce cool and blend in blender. Remove from heat, stir in lemon zest and juice.

Bake chicken at 450°F for 30 minutes. Remove from oven, flip chicken to other side, spoon sauce on chicken.
Bake at 450°F for 10-15 minutes. Toss chicken in sauce, garnish with crushed red pepper flakes, serve.

SPICY ASIAN PEPPER'D WINGS

Baked chicken wings tossed in a spicy Asian-inspired bell pepper sauce and garnished with toasted sesame seeds.

INGREDIENTS:

- 4 pounds chicken wingettes and drummettes
- Black pepper
- Seasoned salt
- Garlic powder
- Onion powder
- Ground coriander
- Toasted sesame seeds

SAUCE

- ¾ cup oyster sauce
- ¾ cup honey or agave
- ¼ cup light soy sauce
- 1 tablespoon cornstarch
- 1/8 cup crushed red pepper
- Toasted sesame seed oil
- 1 medium shallot, diced
- 1 garlic bulb, minced
- 1 ounce ginger (2-3 inches), minced
- 1 yellow bell pepper, diced
- 1 orange bell pepper, diced
- 1 red bell pepper, diced
- 1 ounce basil, chopped

DIRECTIONS:

Preheat oven to 450°F.
Spray a foil-lined cookie sheet with cooking spray. Generously season both sides of chicken with black pepper, seasoned salt, garlic powder, onion powder and ground coriander. Transfer chicken to prepared cookie sheet, set aside in refrigerator.

FOR THE SAUCE
Mix oyster sauce, honey/agave, soy sauce, cornstarch, and red pepper, set aside.
Heat toasted sesame seed oil in saucepan over medium heat. Sauté shallot, garlic, and ginger until fragrant (5-7 minutes).

Add oyster sauce mixture, bring to boil, stir constantly (7-10 minutes). Add bell peppers and basil, stir, bring to boil, cook (7-10 minutes). Remove from heat.

Bake chicken at 450°F for 30 minutes. Remove from oven, flip chicken to other side, spoon sauce on chicken.

Bake at 450°F for 10-15 minutes. Toss chicken in sauce, garnish with toasted sesame seeds, serve.

SMOKED COCONUT LIME WINGS

Baked chicken wings tossed in a smoked coconut sauce and garnished with sweet shredded coconut flakes, lime zest and juice.

INGREDIENTS:

- 4 pounds chicken wingettes & drummettes
- Black pepper
- Salt
- Ground ginger
- Limes, zest and juice

SAUCE

- 1 cup cream of coconut
- 1 cup coconut milk
- 2 teaspoon cornstarch
- 2 tablespoons coconut oil
- 1 cup shredded coconut sweetened, plus extra for garnish
- 2 tablespoons Worcestershire
- ½ teaspoon liquid smoke
- ½ teaspoon ground ginger
- ½ teaspoon vanilla bean

DIRECTIONS:

Preheat oven to 450°F.
Spray a foil-lined cookie sheet with cooking spray, set aside. Generously season both sides of chicken with black pepper, salt, and ground ginger. Transfer chicken to prepared cookie sheet, set aside.

FOR THE SAUCE
Mix cream of coconut, coconut milk, and cornstarch, set aside.

Heat coconut oil in saucepan, add shredded coconut, cook until brown (3-5 minutes). Add cream of coconut mixture, stir. Add Worcestershire, liquid smoked, ground ginger, and vanilla bean. Bring to boil, cook (5 minutes). Remove from heat.

Bake chicken at 450°F for 30 minutes. Remove chicken from oven, flip chicken to other side. Bake at 450°F for 10-15 minutes. Toss chicken in sauce, garnish with shredded coconut, lime zest and juice. Serve with fresh lime slices.

ENTREES

Wasabi Seafood Pizza

Spicy Turkey Burger and Fries

Shrimp Curry Noodles

Cilantro Fish and Poblano Rice

Sweet Pepper Meatball Pasta

Whole Fish and Mushroom Marsala Couscous

Red Wine Lamb Chops/Tacos

WASABI SEAFOOD PIZZA

Asian-style thin crust pizza featuring a sweet honey wasabi sauce, shrimp, crab, scallops, shiitake, colorful sweet peppers, ginger and chopped sesame sticks.

INGREDIENTS:

HONEY WASABI SAUCE
- 1/3 cup mayo
- 2 tablespoons wasabi
- 1 tablespoon honey

CAULIFLOWER CRUST (Or use a premade thin crust)
- 1 cauliflower head, stem removed
- 1 egg
- ½ cup mozzarella
- 1 tablespoon garlic powder
- 1 tablespoon Chinese 5 spice powder
- 1 teaspoon onion powder
- ½ teaspoon celery salt
- ¼ teaspoon smoked paprika
- Toasted sesame seed oil

TOPPINGS
- ¼ pound shrimp, peeled and halved lengthwise
- ¼ pound pound lump crab
- ¼ pound baby scallops
- 1 small shallot, thinly sliced
- 1 garlic bulb minced
- ¼ ounce ginger (1 inch), minced
- 1 ounce shiitake, chopped and soaked in water
- Smoked Gouda, shredded
- ½ cup sweet peppers, sliced
- 1 jalapeño, diced
- Wasabi peas, crushed
- Sesame sticks, chopped
- Crushed red pepper
- Toasted sesame seeds
- Sriracha

DIRECTIONS:

FOR THE CRUST
Preheat oven to 450°F.
Line a pizza pan or baking sheet with parchment paper. Grate or pulse cauliflower in food processor until finely ground (yields 3-4 cups). Cover and heat cauliflower in microwave-safe bowl on high for 8 minutes, let cool.

Strain moisture from cauliflower with cheese cloth.* Transfer cauliflower to large bowl, add egg, mozzarella, garlic, Chinese 5 spice, onion powder, celery salt, and smoked paprika. Mix thoroughly.

Lightly oil parchment-lined pizza pan with toasted sesame seed oil. Work cauliflower mixture into pizza crust circle (9-12 inch diameter), evenly round edges of crust.

Brush crust with toasted sesame seed oil.

Bake at 450°F until crust browns and edges crisp (15 minutes).

FOR THE SAUCE
Mix all ingredients well.

*Removing all of the moisture from the cauliflower is the key to a crispy thin crust.

FOR THE TOPPINGS

Heat toasted sesame seed oil over medium heat in small skillet. Sauté shallot until soft and translucent, add garlic, ginger, and shiitake. Cook until soft (5 minutes), remove from skillet, set aside. Keep remaining oil and browned bits in skillet.

Add shrimp to skillet, cook in remaining oil and brown bits over medium-high heat until halfway pink (5-7 minutes). Remove from shrimp from skillet, set aside.

ASSEMBLE

Evenly spread honey wasabi sauce on pizza crust. Toss lump crab in any additional sauce, set aside. Spread smoked Gouda on crust, top with shrimp. Bake at 450°F until shrimp is completely cooked and opaque (1-3 minutes).

Evenly top with sautéed shallot, garlic, ginger, and mushroom mixture. Add a layer of smoked Gouda cheese, sweet peppers, and diced jalapeños. Lightly sprinkle with smoked Gouda cheese.

Bake at 450°F until cheese is melted (10-15 minutes). Garnish with wasabi peas, sesame sticks, crushed red pepper, and toasted sesame seeds. Drizzle and serve each slice with sriracha sauce (optional).

SPICY TURKEY BURGER AND FRIES

A *classic cheeseburger featuring a spicy turkey patty, dressed with lettuce, pickles, tomatoes, onions, cheddar cheese, "secret sauce" served with home-cut fries.*

INGREDIENTS:

BURGER PATTY
- 1 pound ground turkey
- 1 package hot Italian turkey sausage (about 1.25 pounds), meat removed from casing
- 8 ounce mushrooms, finely chopped
- 2 jalapeños, diced
- 2 eggs
- 1 medium white onion, diced
- 1 garlic bulb, minced
- 1/8 cup Worcestershire sauce
- 1/8 cup liquid smoke
- 1 ounce package Ranch dry seasoning mix
- 1 tablespoon crushed red pepper
- 1 teaspoon chili powder
- ½ teaspoon ground cayenne pepper
- ½ teaspoon black pepper
- ¼ teaspoon salt

SECRET SAUCE*
- ¼ cup mayonnaise
- ½ white onion, finely chopped
- 2 tablespoons spicy ketchup
- 2 tablespoons sweet pickle relish
- 1 tablespoon spicy brown mustard
- ½ teaspoon apple cider vinegar
- ½ teaspoon sugar
- Tabasco sauce, to taste
- Salt, to taste

HOME-CUT FRIES
- 1 large Russet potato, peeled and rinsed
- Buttermilk, cold
- Chicken broth
- Frying oil
- Black pepper
- Salt

BURGER & TOPPINGS
- Burger buns, toasted
- Lettuce
- Pickles
- Tomatoes
- Red onion
- Cheddar cheese
- Secret sauce*

DIRECTIONS:

FOR THE BURGER
Combine all burger ingredients in a large bowl, mix thoroughly. Shape meat mixture into 1-inch-thick burger patties, set aside.

Grease and heat charcoal grill to high, or heat oil in medium skillet over medium heat. Cook patties until browned on each side and internal temperature is 165°F (5-7 minutes each side).

FOR THE SECRET SAUCE
Mix all ingredients well.

FOR THE HOME-CUT FRIES
Cut potatoes lengthwise into ½-inch-thick sticks. In a large bowl, submerge potatoes in equal parts buttermilk and chicken broth. Chill in fridge for 1 hour.

Heat frying oil to 300°F in a large heavy bottomed skillet or deep fryer. Fry potatoes until they begin to golden (5-7 minutes). Remove potatoes from oil, transfer to paper towel-lined plate to cool.

Increase oil temperature to 350°F. Fry potatoes again until golden and brown (5 minutes). Remove from oil and transfer to paper towel-lined plate.

Season with pepper and salt to taste.

FOR THE BURGER
Melt cheddar over patty. Assemble burger with all topping ingredients. Serve with home-cut fries and additional secret sauce.

SHRIMP CURRY NOODLES

One-pot, Thai-inspired shrimp curry noodles with fresh, vibrant veggies.

INGREDIENTS:
- 1 pound shrimp, peeled and cleaned
- Toasted sesame seed oil
- 1 shallot, sliced
- 1 garlic bulb, minced
- ¼ cup ginger, minced
- 3 tablespoons yellow curry powder
- 4 cups low-fat coconut milk
- 4 Roma tomatoes, cubed
- 1 ounce dried shiitake, soaked and sliced
- 1 red bell pepper, chopped
- 8 ounces flat Thai-style noodles (8 ounces)
- 1/8 cup fish sauce
- 1/8 cup soy Sauce
- 1 ounce Thai basil leaves, chopped
- ½ cup cilantro leaves
- Black pepper, to Taste
- Salt, to taste
- Crushed red pepper, to garnish
- Chives, to garnish

DIRECTIONS:
Heat toasted sesame seed oil in large pot over medium heat. Add shallot, cook until tender, stirring occasionally. Add garlic and ginger, cook, stirring occasionally, until tender. Add curry powder, mix well, cook until brown bits begin to form (2-4 minutes). Add coconut milk, stir scraping browned bits from the bottom of the pot. Add shrimp, bring to boil, cook (3-5 minutes).

Reduce to medium heat, add tomatoes, shiitake, bell pepper, fish sauce, soy sauce, and noodles. Cook until noodles become tender (5-7 minutes).

Remove from heat, stir in basil, cilantro, salt and pepper to taste. Garnish with crushed red pepper and chives. Serve immediately.

CILANTRO FISH AND POBLANO RICE

Pan-fried Mexican-style fish dressed in a cilantro lime sauce, paired with spicy poblano rice with jalapeño, corn, beans and lime zest.

INGREDIENTS:

POBLANO RICE
- Olive oil
- 1 onion, diced
- 1 bulb garlic, chopped
- 2 poblano peppers, chopped
- 2 jalapeño peppers, chopped
- 2 cups white rice
- 2 cups chicken broth
- 1 ½ cup coconut milk
- 2/3 cup sweet corn canned
- 2/3 cup navy beans canned
- Cilantro leaves
- Cumin
- Black pepper
- Salt

CILANTRO-LIME SAUCE
- ½ cup olive oil
- 1 cup green onions, thinly sliced
- 1 cup cilantro leaves
- ½ cup lime juice
- ¼ cup jalapeño peppers, chopped
- 1/8 cup soy sauce
- 2 teaspoons vinegar
- Salt

FISH FILLETS
- Fish fillets (catfish, tilapia, or cod)
- Black pepper
- Kosher salt
- Cumin
- Flour
- Frying oil

DIRECTIONS:

FOR POBLANO RICE
Drain liquid from corn and beans. Discard liquid, set corn and beans aside.

Heat olive oil over medium heat in medium-sized skillet. Add onion, cook until fragrant (5 minutes). Add garlic, poblano peppers, jalapeño peppers (add more olive oil if necessary), cook until garlic and peppers become fragrant and soft (7-10 minutes). Add rice, mix thoroughly, continue to cook until rice starts to brown. Pour in chicken broth. Add salt, pepper, and cumin to taste. Bring to boil, let boil until liquid has mostly evaporated. Reduce heat to medium-low, add coconut milk, cover, cook until rice absorbs coconut milk completely. (20-25 minutes, stirring gently every 5-7 minutes).

Remove from heat. Mix in corn, beans and cilantro leaves to taste. Season with additional salt, pepper and cumin to taste.

FOR THE CILANTRO-LIME SAUCE
Mix olive oil, green onions, cilantro leaves, lime juice, jalapeño, soy sauce and vinegar in a medium bowl. Set aside for 10-25 minutes, add salt to taste.

FOR THE FRIED FISH FILLETS
Season both sides of fish fillets with black pepper, salt and cumin to taste. Lightly and evenly coat each side with flour.

Heat ½-inch frying oil in a large skillet over medium-high heat until hot. Add fillets to oil, do not move fillets once placed. Fry fillets until crisp and brown on the bottom (5-7 minutes), flip to the other side and cook until thickest part of the fillet is completely cooked through. Transfer fish to a paper towel-lined plate.

Serve fish with rice, spoon sauce over fish and rice. Garnish plate with lime zest.

41

SWEET PEPPER MEATBALL PASTA

Savory, spicy turkey meatballs in sweet pepper, tomato and mushroom white wine sauce, garnished with shaved parmesan and red pepper flakes.

INGREDIENTS:

MEATBALLS
- 1 package hot Italian turkey sausage (about 1.25 pounds), meat removed from casing
- 1 egg
- 1 medium onion, finely diced
- 1 garlic bulb, minced
- ½ cup freshly grated Romano cheese
- 1/8 cup Worcestershire sauce
- 1 tablespoon dried basil leaves
- 1 tablespoon dried oregano leaves
- 1 teaspoon dried thyme leaves
- 1 teaspoon liquid smoke
- ¼ teaspoon smoked paprika
- ¼ teaspoon brown sugar
- Black pepper
- Salt
- Olive Oil

SAUCE
- Olive oil
- 1 medium shallot, thinly sliced
- 1 garlic bulb, minced
- 1 cup mushroom, sliced
- ½ cup dry Marsala wine
- 1 pound sweet peppers, sliced and divided
- 21 ounces cherry tomatoes, halved
- 1/8 cup capers, drained
- Red pepper flakes
- Tabasco sauce
- Black pepper
- Salt

PASTA
- Pasta (spaghetti, fettuccine, tagliatelle, tortellini, linguine, or pappardelle)
- Shaved parmesan cheese
- Crushed red pepper flakes

DIRECTIONS:

FOR THE MEATBALLS
Mix all meatball ingredients together in large bowl. Shape into 1 inch meatballs.

Heat olive oil in large iron or oven-safe skillet. Cook meatballs in skillet until browned (10-12 minutes). Remove skillet from heat, broil hi on top rack (3-5 minutes), set aside.

FOR THE SAUCE
Heat olive oil in medium sauce pot over medium heat. Sauté shallot until soft and translucent, add garlic and mushrooms. Cook covered (5-7 minutes), stir occasionally.

Add wine, stir, cook until wine reduces by half (7-10 minutes). Add ½ pound sweet peppers, stir, cover, cook until soft (7-10 minutes). Add cherry tomatoes, cook covered until juice forms, stir occasionally (7-10 minutes). Remove lid, bring to boil, cook until liquid reduces (10 minutes). Add capers and remaining ½ pound sweet peppers, mix well.

Season with red pepper flakes, Tabasco, black pepper, and salt to taste. Remove from heat, mix in meatballs and remaining ½ pound sweet peppers.

FOR THE PASTA
Cook pasta according to package instructions.

Serve sauce over pasta, top with meatballs, shaved parmesan cheese and red pepper flakes.

WHOLE FISH AND MUSHROOM MARSALA COUSCOUS
WITH ROASTED CARROTS AND POTATOES

Roasted whole fish drizzled in a lemon butter caper sauce, served with mushroom marsala couscous, roasted carrots and rainbow potatoes.

INGREDIENTS:

MUSHROOM MARSALA COUSCOUS
- 2 cups Israeli couscous
- 2 tablespoons butter
- 1 shallot, chopped
- 1 bulb garlic, minced
- 8 ounces mushroom, diced
- ½ cup Marsala wine
- 1 cup heavy cream
- Rosemary
- Thyme
- ¼ cup honey Dijon mustard
- 1 teaspoon liquid smoke
- 2/3 cup shaved parmesan
- Black pepper
- Salt

LEMON BUTTER CAPER SAUCE
- 2 tablespoons butter
- 5 cloves garlic, minced
- 2 tablespoons capers, drained
- 1 lemon, zest and juice

FISH
- Whole fish, snapper or branzino, cleaned and scored
- Black pepper
- Garlic powder
- Salt
- Garlic cloves, minced
- Rosemary
- Thyme
- Lemon, thinly sliced

CARROTS & POTATOES
- 1 pound whole carrots
- 1 ½ pounds rainbow potatoes
- ¼ cup olive oil
- 1 bulb garlic, chopped
- 1/8 cup fresh rosemary leaves
- 1/8 cup fresh thyme leaves
- ½ teaspoon smoked paprika
- Cracked black pepper
- Pink Himalayan salt

DIRECTIONS:

FOR THE MUSHROOM MARSALA COUSCOUS
Cook Israeli couscous according to package instructions, set aside to drain.

Melt butter in skillet over medium-high heat. Cook shallot until soft and translucent. Add garlic, sauté until soft and fragrant, stir. Add mushrooms, cook mushrooms until they begin to make a liquid, cook until liquid begins to reduce (7-10 minutes). Add marsala wine, increase heat to high, cook stirring frequently until wine reduces to half
(5-7 minutes).

Reduce heat to medium-low, add heavy cream, stir. Add rosemary, thyme, honey Dijon mustard and liquid smoke, stir. Reduce heat to low, add parmesan, cook, stir until cheese melts (3-5 minutes).

Remove skillet from heat, stir in black pepper and salt to taste. Mix couscous into sauce well. Season with additional pepper and salt to taste.

FOR THE LEMON BUTTER CAPER SAUCE
Melt butter in small sauce pan over medium heat. Add garlic and capers, stir, bring to simmer. Add lemon zest and juice to taste. Set aside, let cool to room temperature.

FOR THE FISH
Preheat oven to 450°F.

Generously season whole snapper with black pepper, garlic powder, and salt to taste. Stuff fish with garlic, rosemary, thyme and lemon slices. Bake until fish is cooked through and meat is white (18-20 minutes).

FOR THE CARROTS & POTATOES
Preheat oven to 400°F.

Cut potatoes into halves, soak in water, set aside. Rinse and remove tops from carrots, pat dry, cut into quarters lengthwise, set aside. Combine olive oil, garlic, rosemary and thyme in large bowl, set aside.

Remove potatoes from water, pat dry. Toss carrots and potatoes in olive oil, coat thoroughly. Add cracked black pepper, smoked paprika and pink Himalayan salt to taste.

Transfer carrots and potatoes to iron skillet or oven safe dish. Cover and bake until potatoes and carrots are tender (40 minutes).

Drizzle the whole fish with lemon caper butter sauce and serve with mushroom marsala couscous, roasted carrots and potatoes.

RED WINE LAMB CHOPS/TACOS
WITH PEAR AND FENNEL MINT SLAW

Red wine marinated lamb chops, pan-fried in a spiced cocoa-coffee rub, topped with a refreshing pear and fennel mint slaw, garnished with feta cheese crumbles and served with spicy butter potatoes.
Can be made in an alternative taco variation.

INGREDIENTS:

RED WINE MARINADE
- 4 lamb chops (or 1 ½ pounds of lamb cubes for taco)
- 1 cup dry red wine, cabrenet
- ¼ cup olive oil
- 1 bulb garlic, mashed
- 2 lemons, zest and juice
- 1 shallot, sliced
- ½ ounce rosemary, chopped
- Cracked black pepper
- Kosher salt
- 1 tablespoon cornstarch
- Tortillas, toasted
- Feta cheese crumbles

SPICY COCOA-COFFEE RUB
- ¼ cup brown sugar
- 1 tablespoon medium roast coffee grinds
- 1 tablespoon unsweetened cocoa powder (100% cacao)
- 1 teaspoon cayenne powder
- 1 teaspoon garlic powder
- 1 teaspoon onion powder
- 1 teaspoon smoked paprika
- ½ teaspoon black pepper
- ½ teaspoon cumin
- ½ teaspoon ground ginger
- ½ teaspoon ground mustard
- ½ teaspoon salt
- ¼ teaspoon cinnamon
- ¼ teaspoon red pepper powder

PEAR & FENNEL MINT SLAW
- 1 green pear
- ¼ cup brown sugar
- 3 lemons, zest & Juice
- 1 ounce mint leaves, chopped
- ¼ of a red onion, diced
- 2 tablespoons fresh ginger, minced
- 1 tablespoon fennel seeds
- 1 tablespoon honey Dijon mustard
- 1 tablespoon honey (or agave)
- 1 tablespoon red pepper flakes
- Black pepper
- Salt

BUTTER POTATOES
- 1 ½ pounds gold potatoes, halved
- 4 tablespoons butter
- 1 tablespoon olive oil
- 1 tablespoon black pepper
- 1 tablespoon garlic powder
- 1 tablespoon Himalayan salt
- 1 tablespoon onion powder
- ½ teaspoon cayenne powder
- ½ teaspoon chili powder
- ½ teaspoon cumin
- ½ teaspoon smoked paprika
- Dried chives

*for taco alternative

DIRECTIONS:

FOR THE MARINADE

Season lamb chops with cracked black pepper and kosher salt to taste, set aside.

Whisk together wine and olive oil in a medium bowl. Add garlic cloves, lemon zest, lemon juice, shallot, rosemary and pepper and salt to taste, mix well. Coat lamb in red wine mixture.

Transfer lamb and marinade into a sealable freezer bag. Marinate in fridge for 4-6 hours.

FOR THE PEAR SLAW

Cut pear into short thin sticks, set aside.

Mix brown sugar, lemon zest and juice, mint leaves, red onion, ginger, fennel seeds, honey Dijon mustard, honey (or agave) and red pepper flakes. Add salt and pepper to taste.

Mix in pear sticks coating pear evenly. Cover, chill in fridge.

FOR THE POTATOES
Soak potatoes in cold water for one hour.

Mix black pepper, garlic powder, Himalayan salt, onion powder, cayenne powder, chili powder, cumin and smoked paprika, set aside.

Remove potatoes from water, pat dry. Toss potatoes in olive oil, season with spice mixture to taste, set additional spice mixture aside.

Heat 2 tablespoons of butter over medium heat in large iron or oven-safe skillet. Add potatoes arranging halves in a single layer across the bottom of the skillet.

Add remaining 2 tablespoons of butter, cover with lid, increase heat to medium-high. Cook potatoes covered until tender (20-25 minutes).

Broil potatoes on low heat until potato skins are charred brown and become crispy (5-7 minutes).

Season with additional spice mixture to taste. Garnish with dried chives.

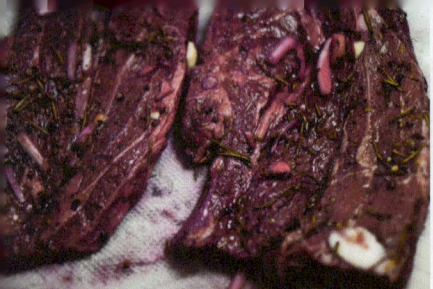  

FOR THE RUB
Remove lamb chops from marinade, discard marinade. Pat lamb chops dry with paper towels, set aside.

Combine all of the rub ingredients in medium bowl. Coat lamb chops in coffee-cocoa rub on all sides.

Melt 2 tablespoons of butter in skillet over medium-high heat. Cook lamb chops over medium-high heat on both sides (8-10 minutes). Remove from heat spoon pan drippings over lamb chops.

ASSEMBLE AND SERVE
Place lamb chop on plate. Drizzle pan drippings on the lamb chop.

Top with pear slaw, garnish with feta cheese crumbles, serve with buttered potatoes.

TACOS

FOR THE TACO ALTERNATIVE
Prepare lamb cubes in red wine sauce (same as lamb chops), marinate in fridge for 4-6 hours.

Prepare pear slaw and coffee-cocoa rub, set aside. Remove lamb chops from marinade, reserve ½ cup of marinade. Add cornstarch to marinade, mix until cornstarch dissolves.

Bring ½ cup marinade to boil over medium-high heat in small sauce pan, stir occasionally until mixture thickens. Remove from heat, set aside to cool.

Coat lamb cubes in rub, pan fry (same as lamb chops). Remove skillet from heat, pull meat into shreds with fork, toss in pan drippings.

BUILD THE TACO - Top tortilla with Lamb meat, drizzle with pan drippings, spoon marinade sauce, then pear slaw. Top with feta cheese crumbles, sriracha, and garnish with red pepper flakes.

DESSERTS

AVOCADO KEY LIME PIE

BOOZY MANGO PEACH COBBLER

DRUNKEN SLOPPY S'MORES

COCONUT LIME–BASIL RUM CAKE

AVOCADO KEY LIME PIE

No-bake smooth and creamy (kind of healthy) key lime pie with an avocado coconut filling, garnished with lime zest, coconut flakes and edible flowers.

INGREDIENTS:

CRUST
- 1 ½ cup graham cracker crumbs
- 1/3 cup sugar
- 6 tablespoons butter, melted

FILLING
- 2 large or 3 medium avocados, mashed
- 8 ounces cream cheese, softened
- 1 (14 ounce) sweetened condensed milk, fat free
- 1 cup sweetened shredded coconut
- ¼ cup agave
- 2 limes, zest and juice
- 2 lemons, zest and juice
- 1 teaspoon vanilla bean paste

GARNISH
- Sweetened shredded coconut
- Edible flowers
- Mango, cubed
- Lime zest

DIRECTIONS:

FOR THE CRUST

Preheat oven to 350°F. In a medium bowl, combine graham cracker crumbs and sugar. Add melted butter, mix well. Press crumb mixture into the bottom and sides of 9-inch pie pan. Bake until crust browns (7-10 minutes). Set aside to cool.

FOR THE FILLING

Beat avocados, cream cheese, condensed milk, agave, lime zest and juice, lemon zest and juice, until smooth. Stir in shredded coconut and vanilla bean paste.
Spoon filling into crust, spread evenly. Garnish with shredded coconut, edible flowers, mango, and lime zest. Chill for 3 hours or overnight. Serve cold.

BOOZY MANGO PEACH COBBLER

Fresh peaches and mangoes bathed in honey whiskey and peach schnapps, and baked under a brown sugar crust.

INGREDIENTS:

MANGO-PEACH FILLING
- 6 fresh peaches, sliced
- 2 large mangoes, cubed
- ½ cup brown sugar
- ¼ cup honey whiskey
- ¼ cup peach schnapps
- 4 tablespoons cornstarch
- 1 teaspoon cinnamon
- 1 teaspoon nutmeg
- ½ teaspoon vanilla beans
- ¼ teaspoon allspice
- ¼ teaspoon Chinese 5 spice powder
- 2 tablespoons butter

BROWN SUGAR CRUST
- 1 cup all-purpose flour
- ½ cup brown sugar
- 1 teaspoon baking powder
- ½ teaspoon salt
- 8 tablespoons butter, cold and cubed
- ¼ cup milk, cold

DIRECTIONS:

FOR THE FILLING

Preheat oven to 425°F. Mix all the filling ingredients (exclude butter) in a large bowl, set aside. Melt butter over medium heat in iron skillet or oven-safe dish. Add peach and mango mixture. Bake until mixture bubbles (12-15 minutes). Remove from oven, reduce temperature to 350°F.

FOR THE CRUST

Mix flour, brown sugar, baking powder, and salt. Cut in cold butter cubes, mix. Add cold milk, mix. Spoon crust batter on top of the filling, cover evenly. Bake until crust is golden brown (40-50 minutes), Sprinkle brown sugar over crust after initial 20-30 minutes. Serve warm.

DRUNKEN SLOPPY S'MORES

Deconstructed s'more with a toffee crust and vanilla vodka marshmallows over fruit compote, almonds, chocolate and graham crackers, garnished with a sliced strawberry, blueberries and mint leaves.

INGREDIENTS:

MARSHMALLOW
- 3 tablespoons gelatin
- 1 cup vanilla vodka, divided
- 1 tablespoon clear vanilla extract
- ½ cup cold water
- 1 ½ cup sugar
- 1 cup light corn syrup
- Powdered sugar

FRUIT COMPOTE
- 2 tablespoons butter
- 1 cup strawberries, quartered
- ½ cup blueberries
- 1/8 cup brown sugar
- 1 teaspoon cinnamon
- 1/8 teaspoon cardamom
- 1 tablespoon vanilla extract

S'MORE
- Graham crackers, chopped
- Milk chocolate bar with almonds, chopped
- Toffee bits
- Strawberries
- Blueberries
- Mint leaves

DIRECTIONS:

FOR THE MARSHMALLOWS
Line bottom and sides of a jelly-roll pan with parchment paper. Lightly coat paper with cooking spray, set aside.

Combine gelatin, 1/2 cup vodka and vanilla in a large bowl. Let sit for 15 minutes. Mix water, sugar and corn syrup over medium high heat, stir constantly. Bring to boil, stop stirring. Keep on high heat until mixture reaches 250°F, remove from heat.

Pour hot mixture into gelatin mix, beat immediately with electric beater on high speed until liquid turns white and forms peaks (10 minutes). Add 1/2 cup vodka, beat until thoroughly mixed. Transfer to jelly-roll pan, freeze overnight.

Cover work surface with powdered sugar. Flip marshmallow out of pan onto surface. Coat marshmallow with powdered sugar. Coat a knife with cooking spray, cut marshmallow into cubes. Coat each cube with powdered sugar on all sides.

FOR THE FRUIT COMPOTE
Melt butter over medium heat. Add strawberries, blueberries, brown sugar, cinnamon and cardamom. Stir, bring to simmer. Remove from heat, stir in vanilla extract.

ASSEMBLE AND SERVE
In a 6-ounce oven-safe ramekin, add enough graham crackers to cover bottom of ramekin. Layer chocolate bar pieces on top of graham crackers. Add extra almond slices if desired. Spoon fruit compote on top of chocolate bar pieces. Layer toffee bits on top of fruit compote. Place vanilla vodka marshmallow on top of toffee bits. Add toffee bits on top of marshmallow. Broil on low on top rack until marshmallow melts (3-5 minutes).

FOR THE GARNISH
Slice a strawberry without fully cutting through the berry. Gently spread the slices, place on top. Add a blueberry and mint leaf. Serve hot.

COCONUT LIME-BASIL RUM CAKE

Caribbean-inspired coconut rum-soaked cake, glazed in a refreshing rum-spiked lime basil icing.

INGREDIENTS:

CAKE
- 2 ¼ cup cake flour
- 1 ¾ cup sugar
- 1 (3.4 ounce) pouch coconut pudding
- 2 ¼ teaspoon baking powder
- ½ teaspoon salt
- ¼ cup coconut oil, melted
- 5 tablespoons butter, melted
- 4 eggs, room temperature
- ¾ cup coconut milk
- ½ cup coconut rum
- ¼ cup cream of coconut
- 2 teaspoon coconut extract
- 2 teaspoons rum extract
- ½ teaspoon clear vanilla extract

GLAZE
- ½ cup butter
- ½ cup sugar
- 5/8 cup coconut rum
- 1 tablespoon vanilla extract

ICING
- 1 ounce basil leaves, finely chopped
- 2 limes, zest & juice
- 1/2 cup confectioner's sugar
- 3 ounces Philadelphia cream cheese, room temperature
- 3 tablespoons cream of coconut
- 3 tablespoons key lime rum
- 2 tablespoons heavy cream
- 3/4 teaspoon vanilla extract

DIRECTIONS:

FOR THE CAKE

Preheat oven to 350°F. Mix flour, sugar, coconut pudding, baking powder and salt. In a separate bowl, beat together coconut oil, butter, eggs (one at a time), coconut milk, coconut rum, cream of coconut, coconut extract, rum extract and clear vanilla extract. Add flour mixture to wet mixture one half cup at a time until flour mixture is completely incorporated into the wet mixture. Grease a 9 inch Bundt pan. Pour batter into pan, bake until cake tester comes out clean (50-55 minutes). Cool in pan (10-15 minutes).

FOR THE GLAZE

Melt butter over medium heat in small sauce pan. Add sugar, mix well. Bring to boil for 5 minutes, remove from heat. Mix in rum and vanilla extract, set aside to cool. Poke holes in bottom of cake using a toothpick or skewer. Pour glaze on cake, cover, let rest until cake completely absorbs glaze (10-15 Minutes). Invert cake onto serving dish.*

FOR THE ICING

Mix basil leaves, zest of one lime, juice of one lime, confectioner's sugar, cream cheese, cream of coconut, key lime rum, heavy cream and vanilla extract until smooth. Pour icing over cake, garnish with zest from remaining lime.

*Glaze may cause cake to stick to the pan. To release cake, fill a shallow dish with boiling water, place Bundt pan in shallow pan for 5-10 minutes to allow sugar to dissolve and loosen up. Invert cake, gently tapping the top of the pan with a wooden spoon. Cake should release.

COCKTAILS

MARGARITA ON THE ROCKS

BERRY BASIL COCKTAIL

SMOKED ROSEMARY PEACH TEA

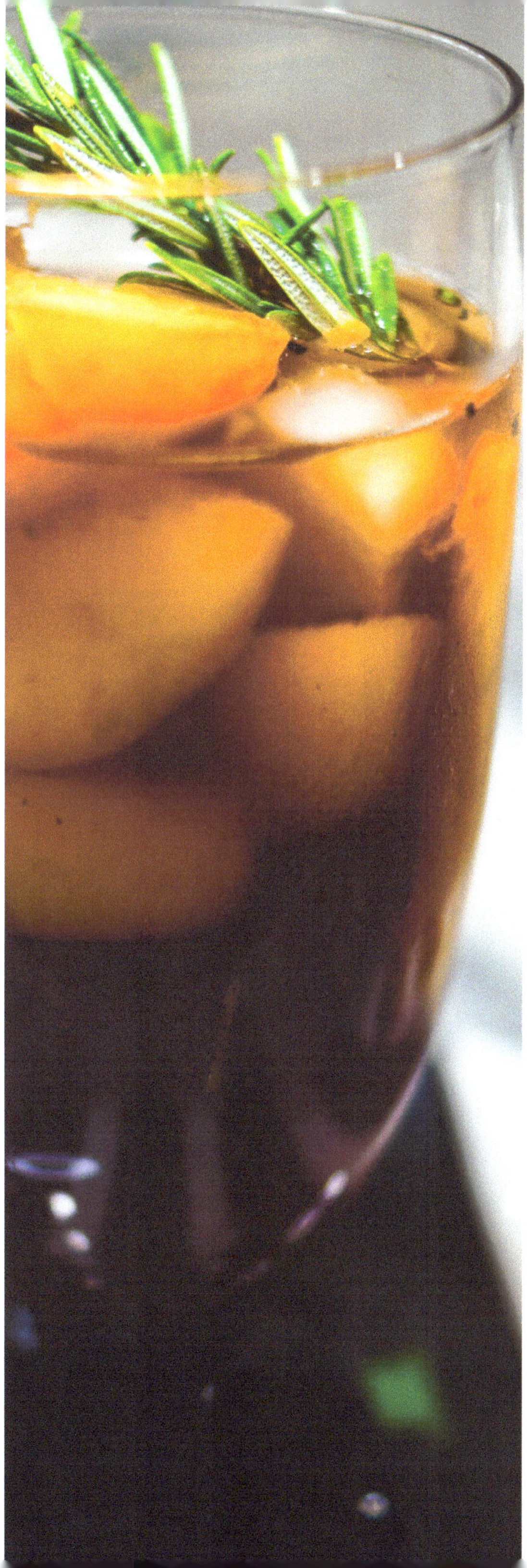

MARGARITA ON THE ROCKS

INGREDIENTS:
- 750 mL Campo Azul tequila, blanco
- 1 ½ cup fresh lime juice (12-15 limes)
- ¾ cup golden light blue agave, plus extra for rim
- 5 limes, zest
- Tajín
- Smoked paprika

DIRECTIONS:
Mix tequila, lime juice, agave, and lime zest. Dip rim of glass in agave, coat rim in Tajín and smoke paprika.

Pour margarita over ice, garnish with additional lime wedge and lime zest.

BERRY BASIL COCKTAIL

INGREDIENTS:
- 6 ounces strawberries
- 3 ounces raspberries
- ½ ounce fresh basil
- 5 ounces ginger beer
- 4 ounces vodka
- 3 ounces grenadine
- 2 limes, juice
- Fresh mint leaves

DIRECTIONS:
Muddle strawberries, raspberries and basil, split between two 8-ounce glasses, set aside.

Mix ginger beer, vodka, grenadine and lime juice, split and pour mixture into glasses.

Slap mint leaves, add leaves to each glass, garnish each glass with additional mint leaves and lime slice.

SMOKED ROSEMARY PEACH TEA

INGREDIENTS:
SIMPLE SYRUP
- 1 cup water
- 1 cup sugar
- 2 tablespoons ginger, minced
- 4 rosemary sprigs

TEA
- 2 cups water
- 4 teabags
- ¾ cup peach whiskey
- ½ cup peach schnapps
- 2 tablespoons almond extract
- Club soda
- 4 rosemary sprigs
- Frozen peaches

DIRECTIONS:

FOR THE SIMPLE SYRUP
Bring water, sugar and ginger to boil in medium sauce pan. Stir until sugar completely dissolves, remove from heat. Light rosemary on fire, let smoke for a few seconds, add to pan, cover. Let steep for at least 30 minutes, set aside.

FOR THE TEA
Brew teabags in water over medium-low heat until liquid is dark. Discard teabags, transfer tea to decanter. Mix in simple syrup mixture, peach whiskey, peach schnapps, almond extract and club soda one cup at a time to taste. Set rosemary on fire, let smoke for a few seconds, add to decanter, cover and let steep.

Pour over frozen peaches, garnish with rosemary sprig.

www.ingramcontent.com/pod-product-compliance
Lightning Source LLC
Chambersburg PA
CBHW041538220426
43663CB00002B/67